WRITTEN BY **PENNY COOKE**   ILLUSTRATED BY **JAROB BRAMLETT**

THE WAKE-UP PRAYER

ISBN 978-0-9909170-7-6

Printed in the United States of America

This Book Belongs to

_____

WRITTEN BY
PENNY COOKE
pennycookeauthor.com

ILLUSTRATED BY
JAROB BRAMLETT
quietstrengthdesign.com

THEA HARRIS PUBLISHING

Thea Harris Publishing Inc.
P.O. Box 7576
Port St. Lucie, FL 34985
www.theaharrispublishing.com

Dedicated to my beautiful grandkids:
Ava, Jayden, Colton, Jensen, Carson, Maya, and Indie

May you always be filled with God's love every morning.

Fill us with your love every morning.
Psalm 90:14 ICB

Open my eyes, pull down the sheet,
climb out of bed, hop to my feet.
Doodles and I sneak down the stairs.
Momma is there, saying her prayers.

"What are you doing on your knees?"
"I'm asking God to bless us, please."
"But I thought praying was for bed."
"Prayer is for always," Momma said.

"But 'Now I lay me' is for night,
just before you turn off the light.
When I wake up, what should I say?
How do you pray when it is day?"

"Come snuggle close and hold my hand.
I'll teach you so you'll understand.
God always wants to hear from you,
at night and in the daytime too."

"Pray when you're glad and when you're sad,
even when someone makes you mad.
When you wake up and start your day,
here is a prayer that you can say."

Now I wake me from my sleep,
from moon and stars and counting sheep.
Lord, thank You for another day
to love and learn and laugh and play.

You kept me safe all through the night,
and brought another morning light.
No matter how the day may be,
I pray that You'll be close to me.

I ask You for a day that's blessed.
Please help me do my very best.
And as I run and skip and swing,
I pray to Jesus' love I'll cling.

May angels guard my every step,
just as they watched me while I slept.
I pray they'll guide me through day's light,
until the day turns back to night.

And when it's time to go to bed,
when teeth are brushed and books are read,
I'll pray the Lord my soul to keep,
and then I'll lay me down to sleep.

"Thank you, Momma, for showing me
how close to God that I can be.
I'll say my morning wake-up prayer
for God to keep me in His care."

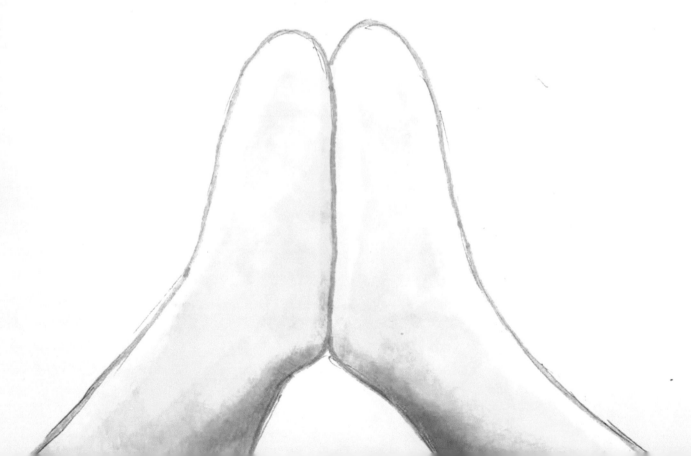

Here is what the Bible says about prayer
(International Children's Bible):

Everyone who continues asking will receive. Matthew 7:8

Always pray and never lose hope. Luke 18:1

Pray at all times. Romans 12:12

Ask God for everything you need. Philippians 4:6

Never stop praying. 1 Thessalonians 5:17

Download your free PRAY coloring page with
"Ten Prayer Tips for Busy Moms & Dads"
at www.pennycookeauthor.com

PENNY COOKE is a certified biblical life coach, mentor, speaker, and podcaster. She is the author of the award-winning book, *Pursuing Prayer – Being Effective in a Busy World,* and many compilations, devotions, and articles. She's a wife to her childhood sweetheart, mom to three, and grammy to seven. Penny's passion is for people to be empowered by prayer, God's Word, and His Spirit for the battles of life. Be encouraged at pennycookeauthor.com.

JAROB BRAMLETT is a husband, father, musician and graphic designer. After working for LiveNation (Tour Design Creative) for over 8 years working with artists such as Paul McCartney and Madonna, Jarob joined strengths with his brother, Joshua, and

together they started Quiet Strength Design. Jarob has a passion for pointing people to Jesus through his art. Check out more of his work at quietstrengthdesign.com.

Printed in the USA
CPSIA information can be obtained
at www.ICGtesting.com
LVRC091917270124
770065LV00088B/494